D1568410

PORTUGAL

ESTER TOMÈ

PORTUGAL

METRO BOOKS
NEW YORK

P. 2: COLORFUL TRAMS RUN ON TRACKS
EMBEDDED IN LISBON'S STEEP STREETS.
OPPOSITE: PRAIA DE CARVOEIRO,
THREE MILES (FIVE KILOMETERS) SOUTH
OF LAGOS, IN ALGARVE, IS A CHARMING
FISHING VILLAGE CENTERED AROUND
A SMALL COVE SHIELDED BY A CLIFF.
IN RECENT YEARS IT HAS BECOME
AN INCREASINGLY POPULAR TOURIST
DESTINATION.

OPPOSITE: THE IMPOSING DISCOVERIES MONUMENT WAS CREATED IN 1960 TO COMMEMORATE THE FIVE HUNDREDTH ANNIVERSARY OF THE DEATH OF PRINCE HENRY THE NAVIGATOR AND TO HONOR FOURTEENTH- AND FIFTEENTH-CENTURY PORTUGUESE EXPLORERS. THE MONUMENT SITS ON THE TAGUS RIVER. FROM THE TOP, YOU CAN ENJOY AN EXPANSIVE VIEW OF THE CITY OF LISBON.

OPPOSITE: HOUSES IN THE CITY OF
PORTO ALONG THE DOURO RIVER ARE
DECORATED WITH LIVELY COLORS AND
INTRICATE *AZULEJOS*.

PP. 10-11: PRAÇA DO COMÉRCIO IN
LISBON. THIS ONCE WAS THE ENTRANCE
TO THE CITY FOR THOSE ARRIVING ON
THE TAGUS RIVER.

PP. 12-13: PORTUGAL IS KNOWN FOR
ITS *AZULEJOS*, GLAZED CERAMIC TILES.
THE SÃO BENTO RAILWAY STATION IN
PORTO PROVIDES MANY FINE EXAMPLES
AND ILLUSTRATES THIS ART FORM'S
ABILITY TO COMBINE FUNCTION AND
DECORATIVE STYLE.

PP. 14-15: MANY OF THE TERRACED
VINEYARDS ON THE SLOPES OF THE
DOURO RIVER VALLEY GROW GRAPES
FOR PORT. PINHÃO IS ONE OF THE
MAJOR TOWNS KNOWN FOR PRODUCTION
OF THIS FORTIFIED WINE.

PP. 16-17: THE FORT OF SÃO JOÃO
BAPTISTA IS LOCATED ON THE ISLAND
OF BERLENGA GRANDE, PART OF THE
BERLENGAS ARCHIPELAGO OFF THE
COAST OF PENICHE. MUCH OF THE
ISLAND IS PROTECTED AS PART OF A
NATURAL PARK WITH ASTOUNDING
LOCAL FLORA AND FAUNA.

PP. 18-19: IN PORTO, HOUSES STAND
SHOULDER TO SHOULDER ALONG THE
DOURO RIVER, THEIR FACES LINED WITH
CHARACTER.

PP. 20-21: PRAIA DA AMOREIRA
IS ONE OF THE PRETTIEST BEACHES
IN THE ALGARVE REGION. ITS ROCK
FORMATIONS ARE UNUSUAL AND
EVOCATIVE.

METRO BOOKS
New York

An Imprint of Sterling Publishing Co., Inc.
1166 Avenue of the Americas
New York, NY 10036

First edition © 2015 Sassi Editore Srl

ISBN 978-1-4351-6809-1

For information about custom editions, special sales, and premium and corporate purchases, please contact Sterling Special Sales at 800-805-5489 or specialsales@sterlingpublishing.com.

Manufactured in China

2 4 6 8 10 9 7 5 3 1

www.sterlingpublishing.com

© Texts, Ester Tomè
Translator: Natalie Danford

CONTENTS

ISLANDS

THE AZORES

- Corvo
- Flores
- Graciosa
- Terceira
- Faial
- Pico
- São Jorge
- São Miguel

Ponta Delgada

- Santa Maria

MADEIRA

- Porto Santo
- Madeira

Funchal

- Islas Desertas

Viana do Castelo

MINHO

- Braga

BRAGANÇA
- Bragança

TRÁS-OS-MONTES

DOURO

- Porto

- Vila Real

NORTHERN PORTUGAL

- Aveiro
- Viseu
- Guarda

THE BEIRAS

- Coimbra

CENTRAL PORTUGAL

- Leiria

ESTREMADURA

- Castelo Branco

RIBATEJO

- Santarém

- Portalegre

LISBON

- Lisbon

- Setúbal

- Évora

SETÚBAL

ALENTEJO

- Beja

SOUTHERN PORTUGAL

ALGARVE

- Faro

NORTHERN PORTUGAL
CENTRAL PORTUGAL
SOUTHERN PORTUGAL
ISLANDS
------- PORTUGUESE DISTRICTS
• DISTRICT CAPITALS

INTRODUCTION

Portugal, located in the westernmost part of Europe on the Atlantic coast, has a rich history and was one of the first places settled in the Old World. The country has been independent since 1140 and has many interesting cultural traditions, some of which reflect its great national pride in its emancipation from its neighbor, Spain. Portugal is small in size, less than 36,000 square miles (92,000 square kilometers), and has only ten million residents. Yet it is packed with beautiful and alluring places to visit. Its varied landscape differs from region to region: valleys, woods, and many bodies of water in the interior are complemented by coastal landscapes with sandy beaches and steep cliffs. In addition to this natural beauty, Portugal boasts an interesting history that has left a legacy of imposing palaces and churches. It is, in short, a country small in physical size, but with a large personality.

Due to its geographical position on the ocean, Portugal was once a great maritime power. It expanded by acquiring colonies on almost every continent. (All were decolonized by 1975.) Today, Portugal retains only two of these former colonies: the Azores archipelago, consisting of nine small volcanic islands in the Atlantic, and the Madeira archipelago, off the coast of Morocco.

Two large rivers have shaped the country's history: the Tagus River and the Douro River. Both originate in Spain and run to the Atlantic Ocean. The Douro River valley, lined with regular rows of grapevines grown on terraces, is visually stunning countryside. This is where the grapes are grown to make Port, Portugal's justly famous fortified wine. The broad Tagus River winds slowly through the heart of Portugal. Its curved path has created large areas that are extremely fertile and provide excellent grazing land for the horses and bulls used for bullfighting. Portugal's largest cities, Lisbon and Porto, are located on these rivers.

Lisbon, the capital, is a modern Western metropolis with many museums and art galleries. Porto, the country's second largest city, is more business driven. The remaining cities and towns in Portugal are notably less developed. The nation is rife with small fishing villages along the Atlantic, medieval villages and towns in its valleys and hills, and great swathes of woods, vineyards, and fields where crops are grown. The Tagus cuts a line through the center of the country that creates two areas separated by more than geography. To the north, the population is largely Celtic and Germanic, while the southern area was first inhabited by Romans and then by Moors, and today its culture still reflects those Mediterranean roots.

Portuguese people are known for being reserved, with a distinctive cordial and gracious yet removed style. They are filled with nostalgia for their glorious past as reflected in a kind of collective national melancholy known as *saudade*. The country is also deeply Catholic. In the north, crucifixes and small altars to the saints appear above the doors of many homes, cafes, and stores. Devotion to Our Lady of Fatima and the many festivals celebrating local patron saints, *romarias*, are a key part of social life in Portugal.

Portugal is also known as the birthplace of famous literary works, including "Os Lusíadas" by the poet Luís Vaz de Camões in the sixteenth century and the nineteenth-century novels of José Maria de Eça de Queirós. The country is a musical powerhouse as well, particularly recognized for its famous fado music, a source of both cultural identity and national pride.

While today Portugal is, obviously, part of the modern world, there is a strong tendency among the Portuguese to look back nostalgically at the Age of Discovery, when Portuguese culture reached its peak in many ways. That period began in 1415 with the invasion of the city of Ceuta in North Africa. Portuguese explorers then made long journeys across the Atlantic and along the western coast of Africa, with the dual goal of vanquishing Islam and expanding their market for trade. Slaves and gold brought Portugal great wealth, but the real turning point came when Vasco da Gama reached India in 1498, and the Spice Route came under Portuguese control. Later discoveries in Brazil and across several continents made Portugal a dominant force in trade, with Spain its only true rival for many years.

Unique and eye-catching Manueline architecture—so named because it flourished during the reign of Manuel I in the sixteenth century—is a Portuguese signature. That style, also known as late Gothic Portuguese, drew many motifs from nautical traditions. The armillary sphere, a tool

Pp. 22-23: Caldeira das Sete Cidades crater lake enjoys a lush green setting on the island of São Miguel in the Azores.
Opposite: The Vasco da Gama Bridge over the Tagus in Lisbon, finished in 1988, is more than ten miles (seventeen kilometers) long, making it Europe's longest bridge.
Pp. 28-29: The eclectic Palácio da Pena sits on the tallest peak in the Serra de Sintra, near Lisbon, and combines various architectural styles.

used to determine the position of the stars, and the emblem of Manuel I, the cross of the Knights Templar (which also appeared on the sails and flags of ships, as the king financed early phases of exploration), appear frequently, as do twisted ropes, often in the form of columns. Works of traditional Portuguese architecture combine these elaborate motifs with features similar to those of the Italian Renaissance.

Another decorative feature indigenous to Portugal are *azulejos*, painted ceramics that also exhibit a strong maritime influence. These tiles cover walls, floors, and ceilings. They were actually a Moorish invention originally, but in the sixteenth century Portugal began to produce its own tiles, and it soon achieved results that were without compare in the rest of Europe. The blue and white tiles from the baroque period are the best known, but many different types are created in different areas, and even today small artisanal workshops make tiles in many parts of Portugal.

Portugal's cities boast impressive architecture, and its countryside offers some of the prettiest landscapes in the world, but its small towns and villages should not be overlooked. Carved and shaped by natural phenomena, they are a shining example of the use of local raw materials, and yet another attractive feature of this small yet mighty nation.

LISBON AND CENTRAL PORTUGAL

LISBON – THE COAST – ESTREMADURA – RIBATEJO – THE BEIRAS

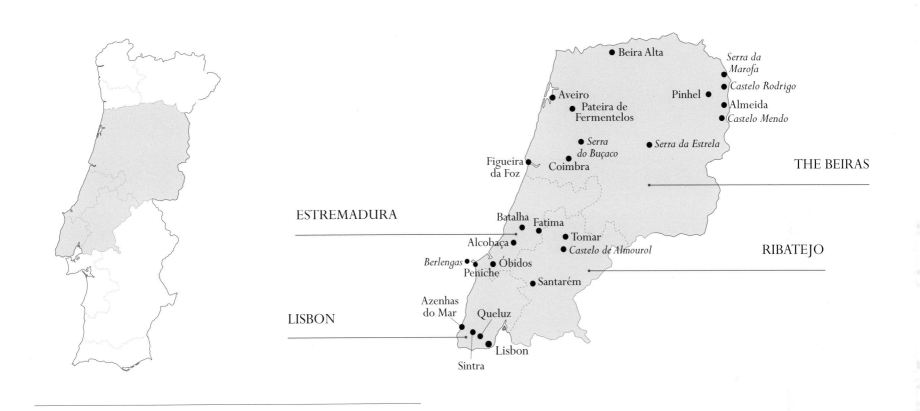

LISBON

Lisbon, Portugal's capital, sits on the banks of the Tagus not too far from the shores of the Atlantic. It is Europe's westernmost city, and it has a distinctive flavor all its own. In 1755, an earthquake destroyed Lisbon, which was then rebuilt with a consistent architectural style that still exists today. The earthquake also inspired many famed works of literature, several of which contemplated the question of whether the natural disaster was divine punishment. These include Voltaire's famous "Poem on the Lisbon Disaster," which laments that man, weak and powerless, is condemned to live a life of desperation.

The city is located on seven hills on the right bank of the Tagus, gifting it with fantastic views. The city follows the twists of the river until it branches off into the Mar da Palha, and each turn of the waterway offers gorgeous scenery full of miradouros, or terraces and belevederes dotted with towers and sloping down Portugal's hillsides. The sense of space is amplified by two spectacular bridges: the 25 de Abril Bridge and the Vasco da Gama Bridge. The latter, built in 1998, is seventeen kilometers (ten and a half miles) long, making it the longest bridge in Europe. The city's various neighborhoods form a dense network laced with narrow cobblestone streets, some of which slope at surprisingly sharp angles. Trams and funiculars crisscross the city. Since the Age of Discovery, Lisbon has been a large commercial center; it has also preserved its character as a port city. The Belém neighborhood at the mouth of the Tagus is lushly green and open and contains museums and a characteristic riverside promenade. It is this area's buildings,

P. 30: THE CLOISTER OF THE CHURCH OF SÃO VICENTE DE FORA IN THE ALFAMA NEIGHBORHOOD IS DECORATED WITH MAGNIFICENT *AZULEJOS* DEPICTING EPISODES IN THE HISTORY OF SEVENTEENTH-CENTURY LISBON.
OPPOSITE: SÃO JORGE CASTLE OVERLOOKS THE ALFAMA NEIGHBORHOOD IN LISBON.
PP. 34-35: THE MODERN GARE DO ORIENTE STATION NEXT TO THE PARK OF NATIONS IN LISBON IS THE CITY'S TRANSPORTATION HUB. DESIGNED BY SPANISH ARCHITECT SANTIAGO CALATRAVA, IT WAS COMPLETED IN 1998 IN TIME FOR THAT YEAR'S EXPO.

OPPOSITE: THE CHURCH OF SANTA ENGRÁCIA SITS IN A LOFTY POSITION IN LISBON, MAKING ITS DOME VISIBLE FROM ALMOST EVERYWHERE AROUND THE CITY. THE CHURCH SERVES AS A PANTHEON THAT HOUSES THE TOMBS OF NATIVES WHO EARNED GLORY AND FAME DURING THE ERA OF EXPLORATION, INCLUDING CAM LUÍS DE CAMÕES, PRINCE HENRY THE NAVIGATOR, AND VASCO DA GAMA

however, that are its true gems. Belém Tower, an ancient tower and still a symbol of Portugal's maritime strength, was built from 1515 to 1521 by order of King Manuel I. It stands in the middle of the Tagus in order to guide sailors en route to the Americas and the Indies. Its architecture combines Manueline and Renaissance styles. Carved ropes, Moorish turrets, battlements embellished with crosses of the Order of Christ, and armillary spheres are intertwined with Renaissance loggias inspired by Italian architecture. A statue of the Virgin and Child that faces the water was meant to offer protection to sailors departing on long journeys.

Another splendid example of Manueline architecture and the opulence typical of Lisbon during the Age of Discovery is the Jerónimos Monastery. King Manuel I ordered the monastery built in 1501, after Vasco da Gama returned from his expedition to India. The project was funded with money from the spice trade, deriving from the taxes the Portuguese charged on spices, precious gems, and gold. The Hieronymites owned the monastery until 1834, when their religious order disbanded.

The Padrão dos Descobrimentos, or Discoveries Monument, is another homage to Portuguese explorers found in this neighborhood. The modern outdoor sculpture was commissioned in 1960 under the Salazar regime to mark the five hundredth anniversary of the death of Prince Henry the Navigator. The angular sculpture resembles a caravel ship. It stands fifty-two meters (170 feet) tall and includes figures representing navigators, kings, cartographers, poets, and painters. An enormous inlaid compass rose on the north side shows the routes charted by navigators.

The Alfama neighborhood—the name derives from the Arabic al-hamma, or "hot springs"—is Lisbon's oldest and sits on the other side of the city. During the Moorish period, the walls of the castles formed the outer border of the city, but during the Middle Ages, wealthier residents, fearing earthquakes, moved west and left this area to fishermen and the less well-off. Today there is no trace of the Moorish houses of the era, but Alfama is still laid out like a kasbah: houses stand shoulder to shoulder along steep streets and interlinked staircases. Clotheslines are strung across narrow alleys. São Jorge Castle on a hill to the east overlooks the entire city. This building dates back to the time of the Visigoths in the fifth century, but during the Moorish period it was expanded, and then the royal family of Portugal expanded it further and used it as a royal residence. Vasco da Gama was welcomed back to Portugal here by King Manuel I when he returned from the Indies in 1499. To the east of Alfama is the Lisbon Cathedral with its two bell towers and a rose window. To the northeast the characteristic domes of the Church of Santa Engrácia and the towers of the Church of São Vicente de Fora dominate the skyline. Alfama is also home to many traditional taverns where the national music of Portugal, fado, is performed. Fado (the word means "fate") is a melancholy version of the blues that reflects the rhythms and movements of African slaves, traditional Arab songs, and local folk traditions.

Baixa, meaning "lower district," is the commercial heart of Lisbon and its most animated area. The center of this neighborhood is dominated by Rossio Square, a large open space and the city's main square and meeting place. After the 1755 earthquake, downtown Lisbon was completely rebuilt by the Marquis of Pombal, who followed a very rigid street grid and connected the Praça do Comércio on the banks of the Tagus to lively Rossio Square. He commissioned neoclassical buildings—all with the same architecture—built on its streets and installed stores and workshops on their ground floors. The full name of Rossio Square is Praça de Dom Pedro IV, an homage to Pedro IV of Portugal, the first emperor of an independent Brazil. These days, the square is lined with cafes and pastelarias, and the Teatro Nacional Dona Maria II stands along its northern side. The neogothic Elevador de Santa Justa was designed in the late 1800s by Frenchman Raoul Mesnier du Ponsard, who apprenticed with Alexandre Gustave Eiffel. The elegant elevator has two cabins decorated with filigree and ironwork, and it connects this neighborhood to Largo do Carmo. At the top a terrace with a café offers a striking view of the entire city.

The Bairro Alto district was completely reshaped by the grid layout established in the sixteenth century; today it is one of the loveliest areas of Lisbon. Once a refuge for well-off residents who left Alfama in the 1800s, when the area declined and became somewhat dangerous, today it is a popular and busy place filled with nightclubs, cafés, and restaurants,

PP. 38-39: THE CONVENTO DO CARMO ATOP A HILLSIDE IN BAIRRO ALTO WAS DESTROYED BY AN EARTHQUAKE IN 1755 THAT LEVELED MUCH OF THE CAPITAL CITY. OPPOSITE: THE FAMED BELÉM TOWER IN BELÉM EXEMPLIFIES PORTUGAL'S FAMED MANUELINE STYLE AND IS EMBLEMATIC OF THE COUNTRY'S PROMINENCE DURING THE AGE OF DISCOVERY.

PP. 42-43: A VIEW OF JERÓNIMOS MONASTERY FROM ATOP THE DISCOVERIES MONUMENT. THE MONASTERY WAS DESIGNED BY ARCHITECT DIOGO DE BOITACA IN SIXTEENTH-CENTURY MANUELINE STYLE. IT IS LOCATED IN LISBON'S BELÉM NEIGHBORHOOD.

P. 44: THE CLOISTER OF THE JERÓNIMOS MONASTERY IS A TRIUMPH OF MANUELINE STYLE WITH ITS MANY CARVINGS AND LACY STONEWORK. IT WAS DESIGNED BY JOAO DE CASTILHO.

P. 45: THE VAULTS AND COLUMNS OF THE CLOISTER IN LISBON'S JERÓNIMOS MONASTERY ARE ELABORATELY CARVED WITH LEAVES, EXOTIC ANIMALS, AND NAUTICAL SYMBOLS.

OPPOSITE: ONE OF LISBON'S
SIGNATURE YELLOW TRAMS CLIMBS THE
CITY'S STEEP COBBLESTONE STREETS.

OPPOSITE: AERIAL VIEW OF CENTRAL LISBON.

OPPOSITE: THIS CAFE IN THE CHIADO
NEIGHBORHOOD OF LISBON EXUDES
PLENTY OF LOCAL CHARM.
PP. 52-53: PRAÇA DE DOM PEDRO IV,
ALSO KNOWN AS ROSSIO SQUARE, IS THE
BEATING HEART OF LISBON.

OPPOSITE: THIS BAROQUE FOUNTAIN
STANDS TO THE SIDE OF ROSSIO SQUARE;
THE BUILDING BEHIND IT IS THE TEATRO
NACIONAL DONA MARIA II.

as well as numerous casas de fado where live music is performed. The Chiado neighborhood in Bairro Alto, on the other hand, is home to the headquarters of many banks and offices of other large companies and is a high-end shopping district filled with luxurious stores and historic cafés. this was once the preferred neighborhood of the city's writers and other intellectuals, and statues of literary standard-bearers still dot its streets and squares. One such statue depicts twentieth-century poet Fernando Pessoa seated outside Café A Brasileira, the city's most famous café.

The Estrela neighborhood to the northwest is serene and quiet, with tree-lined squares and numerous art galleries. This area features a basilica and the lush gardens of the São Bento Palace. To the south is Lapa, a residential neighborhood with lavish homes and many embassy buildings.

THE COAST, ESTREMADURA, AND RIBATEJO

Just a short distance from Lisbon there are numerous towns and villages with interesting artistic backgrounds and beautiful landscapes that compete ably with the charm of the capital city. The palaces in Sintra and Queluz and the many major religious institutions in Estremadura are all quite close to the city. The coast in this area is dotted with small beaches and fishing villages, while further inland, along the Tagus, there are pastures, orchards, and vineyards. Beiras to the north boasts some of the loveliest and most varied natural environments in the country: vineyards in the wine region, the university town of Coimbra, and the stark plains and fortified cities of Beira Alta and Beira Baixa. The Palace of Queluz is located just outside of Lisbon. This was originally a hunting lodge, but in the eighteenth century it was transformed into a magnificent summer residence for the royal family. Today it is one of the best remaining examples of rococo Portuguese architecture and it is full of sumptuous rooms and surrounded by equally lush gardens. To the west, toward the coast, in the heart of a rocky sierra nestled among woods, streams, and cliffs, sits the appealingly green town of Sintra, home to the Palace of Sintra with its unique cone-shaped chimneys.

Between the Tagus and the Atlantic coast is the Estremadura region, a hilly area with steep-walled valleys and sandy beaches. The fertile flood plain known as Ribatejo runs along the banks of the Tagus. Portugal's

most breathtaking medieval monasteries are located here, and speak to the fascinating and often tormented history that unfolded here.

Estremadura, whose name comes from the Latin Extrema Durii (beyond the Douro, the river that served as a natural southern boundary of the Christian world) is like an open-air museum. When Portugal expanded southward in the twelfth century and seized land from the Moors, that land was entrusted to religious orders. Later, during the Age of Discovery from the fifteenth through the sixteenth century, as great wealth flooded into the nation, large baroque building and renovation projects were financed in this area, and much of the resulting architecture was embellished with Manueline detail. As a result, the region is home to massive royal palaces, pilgrimage destinations, archeological finds, Moorish castles, and beautiful vacation spots.

The abbeys in Alcobaça and Batalha and the modern sanctuary of Fatima are famed religious sites that highlight the critical role religion long played in Portugal. The Alcobaça Monastery is the largest church in Portugal. It was constructed in 1153 and is a UNESCO World Heritage Site. In 1147, King Alfonso Henriques conquered the Moors at Santarém, and he had this church of the Cistercian Order built to commemorate the event. Various other monarchs funded expansions and restoration of the building in the following centuries.

The Monastery of Batalha, a masterpiece of Gothic art and Portugal's signature Manueline style, stands a short distance from Aljubarrota, where King John I of Portugal was victorious in battle in 1385. The monastery is topped by numerous steeples, buttresses, gargoyles, and lacy stonework that depicts not only religious themes, but Portugal's strength as a maritime power.

Construction of the elaborate Convent of Christ in Tomar got underway in 1162. The building has a tangled and fascinating history. In brief, originally it was in the hands of the Knights Templar, who played a key role in the Reconquista, when the Iberian peninsula was reclaimed from the Moors. This enormous building balances atop a tall hill, where it blends Romanesque, Gothic, Renaissance, and Manueline styles. Architects João de Castilho and Diogo de Arruda conceived of its complex yet orderly design.

The coast of Estremadura runs from Beira Litoral to Lisbon. Its white sand beaches and large waves have attracted the world's surfing community, and much of the area along the water has been densely built

THIS PAGE: A STATUE OF PEDRO IV OF
PORTUGAL, THE FIRST EMPEROR OF AN
INDEPENDENT BRAZIL, STANDS IN THE
CENTER OF ROSSIO SQUARE. THE STATUE
IS ALMOST NINETY FEET (TWENTY-SEVEN
METERS) HIGH. THE WOMEN AROUND
THE BASE OF THE STATUE REPRESENT THE
CARDINAL VIRTUES OF JUSTICE, PRUDENCE,
FORTITUDE, AND TEMPERANCE, WHICH THE
EMPEROR WAS SAID TO POSSESS.

OPPOSITE: THE EIGHTEENTH-CENTURY ÁGUAS LIVRES AQUEDUCT IS A STAGGERING THIRTY-SIX MILES (FIFTY-EIGHT KILOMETERS) LONG.

OPPOSITE: THE PALACE OF THE
MARQUISES OF FRONTEIRA IS A SPLENDID
ESTATE BUILT IN 1640 FOR JOÃO DE
MASCARENHAS, THE FIRST MARQUIS
OF FRONTEIRA. LOCATED IN BEAUTIFUL
COUNTRYSIDE NEAR MONSANTO FOREST
PARK, JUST STEPS FROM DOWNTOWN
LISBON, IT HOUSES FABULOUS ANTIQUE
FURNISHINGS AND *AZULEJOS* THAT DATE
TO THE TWELFTH CENTURY.

ABOVE AND OPPOSITE: TWO PHOTOS OF THE SPLENDID ITALIAN GARDENS AT
THE PALACE OF THE MARQUISES OF FRONTEIRA WITH GEOMETRIC MOTIFS AND
FIGURES REPRESENTING THE FOUR SEASONS. A STAIRCASE ON ONE SIDE OF
THE GARDEN LEADS TO THE KINGS GALLERY, A TERRACE FLANKED BY TOWERS
WITH PYRAMID-SHAPED ROOFS. THE MAJOLICA NICHES CONTAIN BUSTS OF
PORTUGUESE KINGS.

OPPOSITE: THE PALACE OF QUELUZ,
JUST OUTSIDE LISBON, WAS BUILT IN
1747 BY ORDER OF KING PEDRO III.
ONCE A HUNTING LODGE, THE BUILDING
WAS LATER TRANSFORMED INTO A
LAVISH SUMMER RESIDENCE.
P. 66: THE PINK WINGS OF THE
PALACE OF QUELUZ CONTAIN A
LARGE GROUP OF PUBLIC AND PRIVATE
SPACES. THEY ALSO PROTECT THE
GARDENS FROM INCLEMENT WEATHER.
THE GARDENS CONTAIN HEDGES AND
STATUES OF ALL SHAPES AND SIZES,
AND SMALL STAIRCASES, POOLS, AND
FOUNTAINS ADD TO THE PALACE'S NOT
INCONSIDERABLE CHARM.
P. 67: THE THRONE ROOM, A
RECEPTION AREA IN THE PALACE OF
QUELUZ, IS DECORATED WITH MIRRORS,
PAINTINGS, AND GILDED DECORATIONS.

up in recent years. Berlenga Grande, seven and a half miles (twelve kilometers) off the coast near Peniche, is an island in the Berlengas archipelago. The natural park here is Portugal's only reserve dedicated to marine wildlife and offers unspoiled natural beauty, including large red-ochre rock formations and crystal-clear waters. The only people who live on these islands are fishers, monks, and the lighthouse keeper.

Ribatejo means "shores of the Tagus," an appropriate name for the area located in the valley of this river. The Tagus runs through Portugal for more than 625 miles (1,000 kilometers). It originates in Spain and empties into the Atlantic Ocean. The Castle of Almourol is located on a small island in the river. A magical structure that looks straight out of a fairytale, this castle inspired the well-known chivalric romance Palmerin of England, which tells the love story of heroic Crusader Palmerin and Polinarda. Legend has it that the castle is haunted by the ghost of a princess whose love for a Moorish servant ended unhappily for all parties involved. To the south along the Tagus is Santarém, the capital of this region. Santarém is known for bullfighting, as well as a curious custom in which local cowherds act out fights with each other. It is also the location for several festivals and fairs.

OPPOSITE: AZENHAS DO MAR, A PICTURESQUE FISHING VILLAGE NESTLED AMID THE CLIFFS NEAR CABO DA ROCA. THE STRONG CURRENTS OF THE ATLANTIC IN THIS AREA FORM SMALL POOLS ON THE SAND.

PP. 70-71: THE EIGHTEENTH-CENTURY MONSERRATE PALACE AS DESIGNED IN AN ARABIC STYLE. THE GROUNDS ARE PLANTED WITH CAMELLIAS AND TROPICAL TREES FROM ALL OVER THE WORLD. THE PALACE WAS NAMED FOR THE SIXTEENTH-CENTURY CHAPEL DEDICATED TO OUR LADY OF MONTSERRAT IN CATALONIA, SPAIN.

PP. 72-73: THE PALACE OF SINTRA STANDS IN THE CENTER OF THE TOWN OF SINTRA, JUST TWENTY-FIVE MILES (FORTY KILOMETERS) FROM LISBON. ITS TWO CONICAL CHIMNEYS SERVED AS A KITCHEN EXHAUST SYSTEM.

The Beiras

The cool and green north of Portugal and the warmer southern portion of the country are separated by an area known as the Beiras, which stretches from the border with Spain to the east and the ocean to the west. This area has some of the most evocative—and least crowded—spots in the country. In the western portion there are several lively towns that are pleasant to visit, such as Aveiro, Coimbra, and Figueira da Foz, while in the east along the Spanish border there are numerous fortresses and castles, defensive structures that date back to the Middle Ages.

Aveiro was originally a seaport, but today it has developed into a fairly extensive industrial city. An original network of canals in the center has been preserved, earning it the nickname "the Venice of Portugal." To the south is Coimbra, Portugal's third largest city. At one time Coimbra was the country's capital and the site of its royal palace, and it is still considered an important city in terms of Portugal's history and culture. Coimbra is also home to a very old university, the most prestigious in the country. It was founded in 1537, when it

Opposite: Built circa 1890, Quinta da Regaleira is an evocative and elaborate building in Sintra created to serve as a private residence. It references a rich array of historical eras and religious symbols, as well as occult and mystical motifs. Italian architect and set designer Luigi Manini designed it for António Augusto Carvalho Monteiro.

OPPOSITE: THE DOMINICAN BATALHA
MONASTERY (OFFICIALLY MOSTEIRO DE
SANTA MARIA DA VITÓRIA) IS ON THE
UNESCO WORLD HERITAGE SITE
LIST AND IS A MASTERFUL COMBINATION
OF GOTHIC AND MANUELINE
ARCHITECTURE. ENORMOUS PILLARS
AND VERTICALLY ORIENTED DECORATIONS
COVER THE MAIN FACADE.
PP. 78-79: THE GOTHIC ARCHES IN
THE ROYAL CLOISTER OF THE BATALHA
MONASTERY ARE EMBELLISHED WITH
MANUELINE TRACERY THAT GIVE IT A
LIGHT AND AIRY LOOK. CROSSES OF
THE ORDER OF CHRIST AND ARMILLARY
SPHERES, BOTH SYMBOLS OF PORTUGAL'S
GLORY DAYS OF EXPLORATION, ARE
COMBINED WITH LOTUS FLOWERS AND
VINES OF EXOTIC PLANTS.

moved here from its original location in Lisbon. The university buildings sit atop a hill: the bell tower, the São Miguel Chapel, the Sala do Exame Privado (private exam room), and the baroque Joanina Library are all situated around the Pátio das Escolas, the main courtyard, which has witnessed more than 700 years of academic history.

North of Coimbra, the Buçaco Forest is a fascinating place, part forest and part arboretum. In the early 1600s, Carmelites built a convent here and blazed paths through the thick woods for meditation and prayer and also carved out caves where hermits could practice their faith. In 1810, British and Portuguese forces battled the French in this area, and the monastery was closed. But its statues, fountains, and ruins remain and give this spot a mystical feeling. The eclectic Bussaco Palace Hotel is also located here.

For centuries, Portugal expended much effort to protect its eastern

P. 80: The Convent of the Order of Christ in Tomar is an ancient fort of the Templars and the Order of Christ. Tomar was founded in 1117 by Gualdim Pais.

P. 81: The Renaissance-era Ponte Velha crosses the Nabão River in Tomar. The city's well-preserved historic center features balconies with window-boxes overlooking narrow streets. The Convent of the Order of Christ surveys the city from a hilltop.

Opposite: The evocative ruins of the Castle of Almourol stand on a small island in the Tagus. Legends abound about this quasi-mystical place, including the story of a ghost of a princess who haunts the grounds.

ABOVE AND OPPOSITE: THE SEVENTEENTH-CENTURY FORT OF SÃO JOÃO
BAPTISTA ON BERLENGA GRANDE, AN ISLAND IN THE ARCHIPELAGO OFF THE
COAST OF PENICHE THAT IS HOME TO A NATURE RESERVE WITH A THRIVING
AQUATIC BIRD POPULATION. THE PENTAGONAL FORT WAS ONCE A MILITARY BASE
BUT TODAY IS USED AS AN INN.

THIS PAGE: WHITEWASHED AND PAINTED
HOUSES IN THE TOWN OF ÓBIDOS.
P. 87: CHARMING ÓBIDOS IS
SURROUNDED BY WALLS THAT DATE TO
THE MIDDLE AGES AND WAS ONCE A
MAJOR PORT CITY. IN 1282 KING DENIS
GAVE THE VILLAGE TO ELIZABETH OF
ARAGON AS A WEDDING GIFT.

border from invaders. Proof of this strategy can be found in the many fortified castles still in existence. Many of these were built during the reign of King Denis, which stretched from 1279 to 1325. The buildings are not far from each other, and traveling from one to the next clearly conveys a sense of how frequent and hard-fought such battles were. The Castle of Castelo Rodrigo in the barren and rocky Serra da Marofa mountains is a particularly evocative site; to the south, the fortified village of Almeida is protected by a massive star-shaped castle fortress predominantly seventeenth-century in style. The Castle of Castelo Mendo and the fortified town of Pinhel are also located nearby. The Serra da Estrela is the highest mountain range in Portugal. It is part of an extensive nature reserve with rich and diverse flora and fauna. Sheep still graze in the pastures on these mountainsides and are an important part of life here—both their wool and the cheeses made from their milk are highly prized.

OPPOSITE: A VIEW OF COIMBRA
FROM THE MONDEGO RIVER. THE
BELL TOWER AND OTHER UNIVERSITY
BUILDINGS MARK THE CITY'S SKYLINE.

PORTUGAL

OPPOSITE: THE UNIVERSITY BELL
TOWER IN COIMBRA CAN BE SEEN
FROM EVERYWHERE IN THE CITY.
GENERATIONS OF STUDENTS HAVE KEPT
TRACK OF TIME BY LISTENING FOR THE
CHIMING OF ITS THREE BELLS. THE
PEDIMENT ABOVE THE ARCADE MARKING
THE MAIN ENTRANCE IS DECORATED
WITH THE NATIONAL COAT OF ARMS
AND A STATUE REPRESENTING WISDOM.
PP. 92-93: THE BUSSACO PALACE
HOTEL WAS ONCE A ROYAL PALACE
BUT NOW IS A LUXURY HOTEL. IT WAS
DESIGNED BY ITALIAN ARCHITECT LUIGI
MANINI AND BUILT FROM 1888 TO
1907 IN THE BUÇACO FOREST IN THE
BEIRAS REGION.
PP. 94-95: PATEIRA DE FERMENTELOS
LAKE IN THE AVEIRO DISTRICT.
PP. 96-97: THE COLORFUL BOATS
KNOWN AS MOLICEROS ARE USED TO
GATHER ALGAE FROM THE CANALS IN THE
TOWN OF AVEIRO, ONCE A MAJOR PORT.

OPPOSITE: THESE HOUSES IN AVEIRO WERE PAINTED IN BRIGHT STRIPES SO THAT RETURNING FISHERS COULD FIND THEIR RESIDENCES EVEN IN THE THICK FOG THAT OFTEN CLOAKS THE AREA.

OPPOSITE: COLORFUL *AZULEJOS*
SURROUND AN OLD WOODEN DOOR TO
CREATE A CLASSICALLY PORTUGUESE
PLAY OF TEXTURE AND HUE.
PP. 102-103: PORTO, PORTUGAL'S
SECOND LARGEST CITY, SITS ON THE
DOURO RIVER. THE CITY'S LOVELY
AND CHARACTERISTIC RIBEIRA
NEIGHBORHOOD IS A UNESCO
WORLD HERITAGE SITE.
PP. 104-105: THE RIBEIRA
NEIGHBORHOOD OF PORTO FEATURES
BRIGHTLY COLORED HOUSES THAT LINE
THE DOURO RIVER.

Northern Portugal
Porto — Douro —Trás-os-Montes — Minho

MINHO

Soajo •

Templo de Santa Luzia • Ponte de Lima •

Peneda-Gerês
National Park

Bragança •

Viana do Castelo •

Bom Jesus do Monte

Braga • • Citânia de Briteiros

TRÁS-OS-MONTES

• Guimarães

Serra do Marão

DOURO

Vila Real •

Amarante • • Casa de Mateus

Porto •

Peso da Régua •

• Vila Nova de Gaia

Pinhão •

Porto

The Douro River, whose name means "golden river," flows through the rocks and terraced vineyards of Portugal and into the ocean near the city of Porto. The area in the northeast, near the border with the Galicia region of Spain, is largely natural and includes the mountainous Trás-os-Montes region and the fertile valley—also nourished by the Lima and Cávado rivers—with its acres of vineyards growing grapes to produce Port wine, one of Portugal's most famous traditional products.

Porto is the regional capital and the second largest city in Portugal. This historic city blends past and present in interesting ways. Its history as a center for trade dates back to the time of the Phoenician settlement in this area in the ninth century B.C.E. The Romans then made the town

a stop on their commercial route along the Douro. A local proverb says, "Coimbra studies, Braga prays, Lisbon shows off, and Porto works." Porto first grew rich by supplying crusaders on their way to the Holy Land, then via trade with the colonies, and finally by selling wine, all of which has helped to make and keep it an active business center. It still wears this history proudly: the economic boom of the 1700s, due to wine sales, led to development of an opulent baroque style. Many of Porto's buildings are decorated with friezes, reliefs, gold, and precious wood. But Porto's signature decorative elements are surely the azulejos that can be spotted on almost every wall and that strongly influence the character of the city, which is densely populated by more than one million residents. The narrow alleyways, wobbly cobblestones, and twisting stairways that crisscross Porto are lined with small stores and cafes. These characteristic

OPPOSITE: THE TORRE DOS CLÉRIGOS, A CHURCH BELL TOWER, IS THE TALLEST STRUCTURE IN PORTO AND AT NEARLY 250 FEET (SEVENTY-FIVE METERS) OFFERS SWEEPING VIEWS OF THE CITY AND THE SURROUNDING RIVER VALLEY. BOTH THE TOWER AND CHURCH WERE DESIGNED BY ITALIAN ARCHITECT NICCOLÒ NASONI. ABOVE: A CHIC SHOPPING CENTER WITH A MANICURED ROOFTOP GARDEN SITS NEXT TO THE TORRE DOS CLÉRIGOS.

GRATIA PLENA

OPPOSITE: THE ORNATELY DECORATED
FACADE OF ONE OF PORTO'S
HISTORICAL HOUSES. *AZULEJOS*
GIVE PORTUGUESE ARCHITECTURE A
DISTINCTIVE FLAVOR.
P. 110: IN PORTO, STEEP AND
NARROW STREETS LINED WITH
COLORFUL HOUSES LEAD TO THE RIVER.
P. 113: THE PORTO CATHEDRAL
WITH ITS SYMMETRICAL BELL
TOWERS OVERLOOKS THE RIBEIRA
NEIGHBORHOOD.
PP. 114-115: THE SERRA DO PILAR
MONASTERY SITS SOUTH OF PORTO, ON
THE OTHER SIDE OF THE DOM LUÍS I
BRIDGE.
PP. 116-117: THE DOURO RIVER
VALLEY IS STAGGERINGLY BEAUTIFUL.

byways were left intact even as the central portions of the city were redesigned to allow for the kind of roadways needed in modern times.

Numerous church steeples jut upward from the skyline of Porto. The city is in some ways a study in contrasts: the lovely residential areas around Avenida da Boavista, a bustling downtown, and impressive bridges each contribute a different flavor. The Porto Cathedral sits above the city on Pena Ventosa hill. With its twin gray granite bell towers, this landmark is visible from every angle. Along Rua de Dom Hugo on the southern side of the cathedral is one of Porto's prettiest neighborhoods, Ribeira. The area is a maze of narrow streets and alleyways dating back to the Middle Ages that link the cathedral to the river. The most famous of these streets is the Escadas das Verdades, or "stairs of truth," which opens up to a view of the magnificent Dom Luís I Bridge, built in 1886 by an apprentice to Alexandre Gustave Eiffel to connect the city to Vila Nova de Gaia across the river.

Douro, Trás-os-Montes, and Minho

Further into the interior along the Douro River is a spectacular area filled with vineyards where grapes for Port are grown. Legend has it that this densely planted area is so large that it can be seen from the moon. The Douro runs for almost 560 miles (900 kilometers) here and has carved a winding pathway through steep cliffs of granite and shale, where the layers of rock are clearly visible. The towns of Peso da Régua and Pinhão are located on its banks, as are many *quintas*, or farming estates.

The northern end of this region is punctuated by the picturesque city of Amarante, which is extremely important historically as a home to both poets and painters. Due east is Vila Real, which sits in the foothills of Serra do Marão. The main attraction in this modern city, in addition to the many wineries producing the fortified wine known as Port, is the Mateus Palace, a fantastic example of the Portuguese baroque embellished with the kind of frills and furnishings that were de rigueur for well-off families of the era. The palace was built in the early eighteenth century by Italian architect Niccolò Nasoni and was declared a national monument in 1911. Its rooms and outdoor spaces were conceived to play with light and perspective. For example, the rectangular reflecting pool near the entrance perfectly frames the symmetrical spires of the main facade. The gardens feature carefully manicured hedges and flowerbeds that are in sync with the symmetrical style of the building. In a typically thoughtful touch, tunnels have been carved through the groves of cedar trees so that visitors remain in the cool shade while strolling the grounds.

In northeastern Portugal, between the Tuela and Sabor rivers, in a strategically selected position atop a hill, sits the fortified town of Bragança, built in the twelfth century by order of Fernão Mendez, the brother-in-law of King Alfonso Henriques. The Torre da Princesa, or princess tower, and the fortified towers along the surrounding protective wall give the Castle of Bragança a distinctly medieval character, while the Domus Municipalis, a meeting place for residents, is a rare example of Portugal's Romanesque civic architecture.

The fertile region of Minho sits in the north between the Douro and Minho rivers. This area is considered the nation's breadbasket, and farming and its traditions still impact every aspect of daily life here. Abundant rain and powerful rivers make the area especially fertile. This is where many of the grapes for Portugal's famed vinho verde are grown. The largest cities in Minho are in the southern part of the region and include Braga, the area's major religious site, and Guimarães. Braga is known for its many churches. In the twelfth century it became the archbishopric of Portugal, and it has played an important role in the Church in the centuries since. During Holy Week, this city hosts several large religious celebrations, and in June the city venerates Saint John. The main cathedral in the center of the city houses a collection of religious relics, statues, and *azulejos*. The archbishop's palace is located nearby, though these days the building is used as a library and archives. The Garden of Santa Barbara outside is beautifully maintained. The majestic Biscainhos Museum, housed in what was once an aristocratic residence, is located to the west.

Just outside Braga proper there are several interesting archeological sites, including Citânia de Briteiros, the largest Castro site in Portugal. It contains the remains of 150 stone houses that have been dug up and reconstructed in historically accurate fashion so that visitors can experience a taste of life in the Iron Age.

East of Braga, the magnificent Bom Jesus do Monte sanctuary balances on a hilltop. Its most eye-catching feature is a baroque double staircase, designed in 1722 to link the church to the town below. The stairs are marked by fourteen chapels depicting episodes from the Passion of Christ. In the center is the Escadório dos Cinco Sentidos (Staircase of the Five Senses), with statues, fountains, and symbols meant to appeal to the five senses. The last portion of the stairway is known as Escadório das Três Virtudes and is decorated with allegorical representations of faith, hope, and charity (hence its name, which means Staircase of the Three Virtues). The church itself was built on the site of an earlier sanctuary. In the aggregate, building and staircase combine to create a truly transporting architectural whole.

South of Braga, in the rolling hills, is the city of Guimarães, which was the capital of Portugal beginning in 1139 and has a beautifully preserved historic center. The part of the city that dates to the Middle Ages seems to have frozen in time. Cobblestone streets are lined with houses decorated with statues. A castle with tenth-century walls overlooks the city and adds to its considerable charm.

Viana do Castelo is another city in the Minho region. Located at the mouth of the Lima River and near the coast, since the fifteenth century it has been a major player in fishing and trade. In the 1500s, during the Age of Discovery, Viana do Castelo was extremely prosperous, as many of its residents were shipbuilders or sailors. The city is still filled with lavish buildings decorated in Manueline and baroque style that testify to that great wealth. The city and its surrounding area are a seemingly infinite source of breathtaking views, though there are some factory buildings in the area that mar the otherwise striking landscape. Just outside Viana do Castelo on a hill 980 feet (300 meters) high is the Templo de Santa Luzia. Visitors to the church can climb to the top of the dome to enjoy more fantastic views—indeed, *National Geographic* magazine has deemed the view from here one of the best in the world.

The Peneda-Gerês National Park in the northern part of this region protects 270 square miles (700 square kilometers) of oak, yew, and pine forest populated by wolves, eagles, and other wild animals. The park is one of Portugal's major natural attractions.

OPPOSITE: THE BOM JESUS DO
MONTE SANCTUARY BALANCES ON
A HILLTOP LESS THAN FOUR MILES
(SIX KILOMETERS) FROM BRAGA. THE
IMPOSING STAIRCASE REPRESENTS THE
ELEVATION OF THE SPIRIT.

OPPOSITE: BOM JESUS DO MONTE WAS
BUILT IN THE FIFTEENTH CENTURY ATOP
THE REMAINS OF ANOTHER RELIGIOUS
STRUCTURE.

OPPOSITE: A ROCKY BEACH IN
NORTHERN PORTUGAL AT LOW TIDE.

OPPOSITE: THE SPIRES OF MATEUS
PALACE ARE REFLECTED IN A
RECTANGULAR POOL TO CREATE AN
INTERESTING PLAY OF SYMMETRY.

OPPOSITE: THE TOPIARY HEDGES AT
MATEUS PALACE ARE GEOMETRIC
AND SYMMETRICAL, MUCH LIKE THE
BUILDING ITSELF.
PP. 128-129: A TYPICAL *QUINTA*,
OR FARM, SURROUNDED BY TERRACED
VINEYARDS IN THE DOURO RIVER VALLEY.
PP. 130-131: BRAGANÇA, THE CAPITAL
OF TRÁS-OS-MONTES, WAS NAMED
FOR THE LAST AND LONGEST-RULING
PORTUGUESE DYNASTY. THE MEDIEVAL
WALLED CITY AND ITS FORTRESS
OVERLOOK THE FERVENÇA RIVER VALLEY.

OPPOSITE: LARGO DO TOURAL, ONE OF
THE COLORFUL SQUARES IN GUIMARÃES.

OPPOSITE: THE PALACE OF THE
DUKES OF BRAGANZA IN GUIMARÃES
RESEMBLES AN ARISTOCRATIC FRENCH
RESIDENCE. CONSTRUCTION WAS
BEGUN IN THE EARLY 1400S BASED
ON A DESIGN BY AFONSO I, THE
FIRST DUKE OF BRAGANZA AND THE
BIOLOGICAL SON OF THE MAN WHO
WAS MASTER OF THE ORDER OF AVIS
AND WOULD BECOME KING JOHN I
OF PORTUGAL. THE FAMILY LATER
MOVED TO THE VILA VIÇOSA PALACE
IN ALENTEJO, AND OVER TIME THE
PALACE OF THE DUKES OF BRAGANZA
WAS NEGLECTED. IN 1807 IT WAS
TURNED INTO A MILITARY BARRACKS.

OPPOSITE: The courtyard of the
Palace of the Dukes of Braganza
in Guimarães.

OPPOSITE: VIANA DO CASTELO, ON
THE BANKS OF AN ESTUARY OF THE
LIMA RIVER, IS A QUIET TOWN WITH
IMPRESSIVE BUILDINGS THAT GIVE
TESTIMONY TO ITS PROSPEROUS PAST.
PRAÇA DA REPÚBLICA, A CENTRAL
SQUARE, FEATURES A SIXTEENTH-
CENTURY FOUNTAIN.
PP. 140-141: PONTE DE LIMA DATES
TO THE ROMAN ERA AND CONNECTS
TO THE FIFTEENTH-CENTURY SANTO
ANTÓNIO CHURCH.

OPPOSITE: THE CITÂNIA DE BRITEIROS ARCHEOLOGICAL SITE IN GUIMARÃES.
ABOVE: A WATERFALL IN PENEDA-GERÊS NATIONAL PARK, ONE OF PORTUGAL'S
MOST EXPANSIVE NATURAL ATTRACTIONS. THE PARK IS HOME TO WOLVES, EAGLES,
AND MANY OTHER WILD ANIMALS.
PP. 144-145: THE LIMA RIVER RUNS THROUGH PENEDA-GÊRES NATIONAL PARK.
PP. 146-147: THE ESPIGUEIROS OF SOAJO MADE OF WOOD AND STONE WERE
RAISED ABOVE THE GROUND AND SERVED AS GRANARIES FOR CORN AND WHEAT.

SOUTHERN PORTUGAL

ALENTEJO — SETÚBAL — ALGARVE

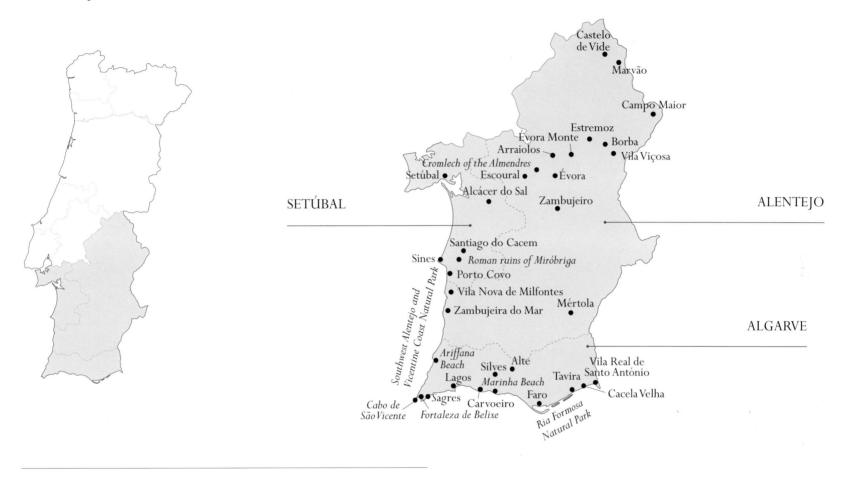

SETÚBAL

ALENTEJO

ALGARVE

ALENTEJO AND SETÚBAL

South of the Tagus, Portugal is largely rural and natural, and in many places surprisingly sparsely populated. The golden fields of wheat and silvery hills and plains of Alentejo stretch as far as the eye can see. The few villages in this landscape date back to the time of the Moors. Here, life seems to slow its pace. The sun and its cycles are a crucial part of the day—the sun's rays land on the stark whitewashed walls of local homes. Algarve, on the country's southern border, is home to gorgeous beaches, golf courses, and other tourist attractions. This is where most of Portugal's large popular beach resorts are located. Algarve is also deeply rooted in

the past, however, and the landscape is dotted with castles dating to the Arab era, and churches and palaces lavishly decorated with *azulejos*.

The Alentejo region stretches from the Tagus valley to Algarve. Sunny and rural, it accounts for approximately one third of the country's land. Fields of wheat, olive groves, and small villages lend a tranquil feel to the area, whose history is narrated by the megaliths known as dolmens and a group of interesting castles.

The city of Évora is located in the heart of Alentejo in a central and strategically fortunate position. Évora played a critical role as far back as the Roman era and was a center for arts and culture in the Middle Ages. Surrounded by a walls of varying heights that were built during the

Roman era, the Middle Ages, and the seventeenth century, the city center represents an unusual layering of the various groups that have inhabited it. The city is known for its cathedral-fortress, beautiful handcrafted goods, a main square lined with Moorish style arcades, and numerous churches and other religious buildings, all of which combine in a rich architectural and cultural mosaic. Praça do Giraldo, the main square, was named for Geraldo Sem-Pavor, or Gerald the Fearless, who in 1165 drove the Moors out of the city. The eastern side of the square boasts marvelous arcades, and the fountain in its center once drew water from the Água da Prata aqueduct, which runs through the northwest part of the city. The aqueduct was designed by Francisco de Arruda, who was also responsible for the Belém Tower. Largo da Porta de Moura, another interesting square, has a Moorish gate on its western side and the gate of the Convento do Carmo on its southern side. The 1556 fountain in the center of the square is an odd combination of Renaissance and futuristic styles with a quirky sphere jutting out of it. The style of the fifteenth-century Saint Francis Church, on the other hand, borders on the grotesque. The bones of nearly five thousand monks are embedded in the walls of the Franciscan Capela dos Ossos, or Chapel of Bones, inside the church, and two mummified corpses hang from the chapel's elaborately decorated ceiling. The entrance is marked by a sign that warns, "We bones are here awaiting your bones."

The area around the city proper is home to many different archeological sites and there are numerous megaliths in the northern hills of the region. The Cromlech of the Almendres is an ancient temple built for worshippers of a sun god. It is oval and made of close to one hundred stones and is located on a hillside amid cork trees and arranged along an axis designed to line up at the equinox. The Escoural Cave has wall paintings that date back to an even earlier time. And the Great Dolmen of Zambujeiro, which has a large entrance and spacious interior, is Portugal's largest megalithic monument.

Several fortified cities are located in the northeastern part of the region. These include Évoramonte, Estremoz, Campo Maior, and Castelo de Vide. Estremoz is one of the loveliest spots in Portugal. The town is surrounded by solid walls. From its perch atop a hill, it overlooks the surrounding countryside and rolling hills of olive groves. The Torre das Três Coroas, or Tower of the Three Crowns (so named in honor of the three kings who funded it) stands out above the skyline. To the east, near the Spanish border, Vila Viçosa and Borba are best known as sources for marble. This "white gold" is widely available in this area and was used not only for elaborate churches, but even in the most humble homes. Vila Viçosa means "fertile valley." After the Moors were driven out in 1226, it became the seat of the Dukes of Braganza and was expanded in order to serve that purpose. Numerous architectural details throughout the city reference the House of Braganza, including friezes engraved on buildings and monuments. The main tourist attraction here is the royal palace with lush gardens and a lavishly decorated and frescoed chapel and library.

To the west, the coast of Alentejo is a pretty ribbon of cliffs and beaches, many of them isolated and untouched. The waters are cold here and subject to strong currents; small fishing villages dot the shoreline. Rice fields and marshes are inhabited by storks, ducks, woodcocks, grebes, and herons. Further inland is Santiago do Cacém, a fortified city built in honor of the Order of Santiago. All the town's steep cobblestone streets lead to a hilltop castle that offers sweeping views of the northern part of the Setúbal peninsula and Sines to the west.

Not far from the city, the Roman ruins of Miróbriga include the remains of ancient thermal baths. The ruins are in a particularly lovely spot in the shade of cypress trees; a few sheep often graze nearby. South of Sines, the coast is part of the Southwest Alentejo and Vicentine Coast Natural Park, which stretches all the way to the Vicentine coast in the Algarve region. Sharp cliffs provide a breathtaking backdrop for the eagles, osprey, and purple herons that live here amid idyllic beaches and untouched coves and a handful of small villages: Porto Covo, Vila Nova de Milfontes, and Zambujeira do Mar.

P. 148: AZULEJOS DECORATE A FOUNTAIN IN ALTE, A TOWN IN CENTRAL ALGARVE.
PP. 150-151: THE CITY OF ÉVORA IN SUNNY ALENTEJO WAS DESIGNATED A UNESCO WORLD HERITAGE SITE IN 1986.
P. 153: ENTRANCE TO THE CHURCH OF THE LÓIOS IN ÉVORA.
OPPOSITE: THE OVAL CROMLECH OF THE ALMENDRES WAS A TEMPLE DEDICATED TO WORSHIP OF THE SUN GOD IN NOSSA SENHORA DE GUADALUPE, IN THE ÉVORA DISTRICT.
P. 156 AND P. 157: THE CASTLE OF MARVÃO WAS BUILT BY KING DENIS IN 1299. IT OFFERS BREATHTAKING VIEWS OF THE SERRA DE SÃO MAMEDE AND THE SPANISH BORDER.
PP. 158-159: THE MEDIEVAL VILLAGE OF MARVÃO SITS AT AN ELEVATION OF NEARLY 3,000 FEET (900 METERS) ON A ROCKY OUTCROPPING NEAR THE SPANISH BORDER, WHERE IT BLENDS IN WITH THE SURROUNDING COUNTRYSIDE.

ALGARVE

Bordered on the north by a chain of hills, Algarve is the southernmost region of Portugal. The name derives from the Arabic al-gharb, or "the west," and this area was at one time a major outpost in the West for the Moors. The land here is very fertile due to the presence of several rivers, and the landscape and culture in this part of Portugal are quite different from those in the rest of the country. The coastline is mild with temperate seas and warm winds from Africa. Due to those conditions and its strategic position, it has long been a sought after piece of land. The Phoenicians, Romans, Moors, and Christians all took possession at one time or another, and today it is "invaded" by hordes of tourists. The inland part of the region is equally charming: villages filled with whitewashed houses, Roman ruins, and exquisite local crafts all contribute to the appeal of Algarve.

The history of this area is nothing short of remarkable: numerous ships launched from the port of Lagos in the sixteenth century as sailors set off to explore, and Prince Henry the Navigator founded a school for navigators and mapmakers in nearby Sagres. Unfortunately, Lagos was the epicenter of a devastating earthquake in 1755 that razed all its buildings to the ground without sparing a single structure. The city we see today was completely rebuilt in the aftermath.

Faro, the region's capital, enjoys a central location on the Algarve coast. East of the city at the mouth of the Formosa river, the Ria Formosa Natural Park contains lagoons, salt marshes, and barrier islands—all typical features of the eastern half of Algarve. The park provides a habitat for aquatic birds, including the purple swamphen, a symbol of the park. This is also a crucial stopover for species migrating between Europe and Africa. Faro itself is an old fishing village that during the Roman era

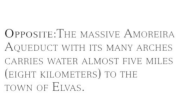

OPPOSITE: THE MASSIVE AMOREIRA
AQUEDUCT WITH ITS MANY ARCHES
CARRIES WATER ALMOST FIVE MILES
(EIGHT KILOMETERS) TO THE
TOWN OF ELVAS.
PP. 162-163: TYPICAL HOUSES IN
ARRAIOLOS ARE WHITE WITH A BLUE
STRIP AT THE BASE. LOCAL LEGEND
HAS IT THAT THE BLUE KEEPS
DEMONS AT BAY.

OPPOSITE: THE ALQUEVA DAM ON THE
RIVER GUADIANA HAS CREATED A LARGE
MANMADE LAKE.
PP. 166-167: THE BEAUTIFUL
COUNTRYSIDE OF ALENTEJO IS KNOW FOR
ITS CORK OAK TREES.

became an important administrative city. It was conquered by the Moors and then conquered in 1249 by King Alfonso III. Today's city does not have any buildings that predate the earthquake, however. The old city center, just east of its small port, is surrounded by walls. The Arco da Vila gate that serves as an entrance to the city was built in the 1800s by order of Bishop Francisco Gomes do Avelar, who is commemorated with a statue on Largo da Sé, the main square in the old city. Orange trees are planted around the square, and two eighteenth-century buildings lend it an imposing tone.

Tavira, Cacela Velha, and Vila Real de Santo António are located in the easternmost part of the coastline. Tavira has graceful Mediterranean-style architecture. Its many churches and elegant buildings are reflected in the Gilão River, which runs through the town. A full thirty-six churches can be found here, and its characteristic four-sided rooftops (handy for

draining the water from the frequent torrential rains that fall in Algarve) lend Tavira a special allure and a historic feeling. Indeed, some of the town's window moldings date back to the Middle Ages.

North of Sagres, the coast is pummeled by cold and often violent ocean currents. The beaches in this windswept area, the Barlavento region, are varied and striking. A string of caves, coves, and beaches that runs from Sagres to Lagos offers lots of opportunity for exploration.

The promontory of Cabo de São Vicente is subject to strong gusts of wind and was once believed to be the edge of the world. To the north, the Vicentine Coast is wild and untamed; much of the area falls under the auspices of the Southwest Alentejo and Vicentine Coast Natural Park. Infrastructure is sparse in this area, but those who do brave the narrow and treacherous winding roads are rewarded with truly breathtaking views of Europe's most beautiful coastline.

P. 168: MÉRTOLA GLIMPSED FROM THE
RIVER GUADIANA.
P. 169: WHITEWASHED HOUSES IN
MÉRTOLA IN THE BEJA DISTRICT.
OPPOSITE: PORTO COVO, A SHORT
DISTANCE SOUTH OF SINES, HAS ROCKY
BEACHES AND AN ANCIENT FORT, BUT ITS
GREATEST ATTRACTION IS THE NATURAL
UNTAMED LANDSCAPE.

OPPOSITE: COLORFUL CERAMIC DISHES AND OTHER ITEMS LEND A DECORATIVE TOUCH TO A STORE IN ALGARVE.
PP. 174-175: TRADITIONAL WHITE AND BLUE *AZULEJOS* ARE ALWAYS EVOCATIVE.

OPPOSITE: THE CABO DE SÃO
VICENTE PROMONTORY JUTS INTO THE
ATLANTIC AND IS BATTERED BY STRONG
WINDS. DURING THE MIDDLE AGES,
THIS WAS BELIEVED TO BE THE EDGE
OF THE WORLD.
PP. 178-179: THE RUINS OF
FORTALEZA DE BELIXE, ALGARVE.

OPPOSITE: THIS STURDY FORT IN SAGRES WAS BUILT ON CLIFFS OVERLOOKING THE OCEAN.

PP. 182-183: TYPICAL OCHRE ROCK FORMATIONS IN LAGOS.

OPPOSITE: A CLASSIC FISHING VILLAGE
BALANCES ON THE ROCKS IN CARVOEIRO.
PATHS AND STAIRCASES LEAD TO
GORGEOUS BEACHES AND COVES.

OPPOSITE: MARINHA BEACH IS ONE
OF PORTUGAL'S BEST KNOWN SEASIDE
SPOTS AND ONE OF THE WORLD'S MOST
BEAUTIFUL. THE PORTUGUESE MINISTRY
OF THE ENVIRONMENT HAS DESIGNATED
IT A GOLDEN BEACH BECAUSE OF ITS
OUTSTANDING NATURAL FEATURES.
IT IS LOCATED ALONG THE COAST IN
THE MUNICIPALITY OF LAGOA IN THE
ALGARVE REGION.

INFANTE D. HENRIQUE
1394-1460

OPPOSITE: A STATUE OF PRINCE HENRY THE NAVIGATOR IN SAGRES, ALGARVE.
ABOVE: THE ARCO DA VILA GATE LEADS INTO FARO. COMMISSIONED BY BISHOP
FRANCISCO GOMES DO AVELAR IN THE NINETEENTH CENTURY, IT WAS DESIGNED
BY ITALIAN ARCHITECT FRANCESCO SAVERIO FABRI AND COMPLETED IN 1812.
THE NICHE ABOVE THE ARCH CONTAINS A STATUE OF SAINT THOMAS AQUINAS. IT
IS ONE OF MANY FABULOUS NEOCLASSICAL ITALIAN ITEMS IN THE ARCHITECTURAL
REPERTOIRE OF ALGARVE.

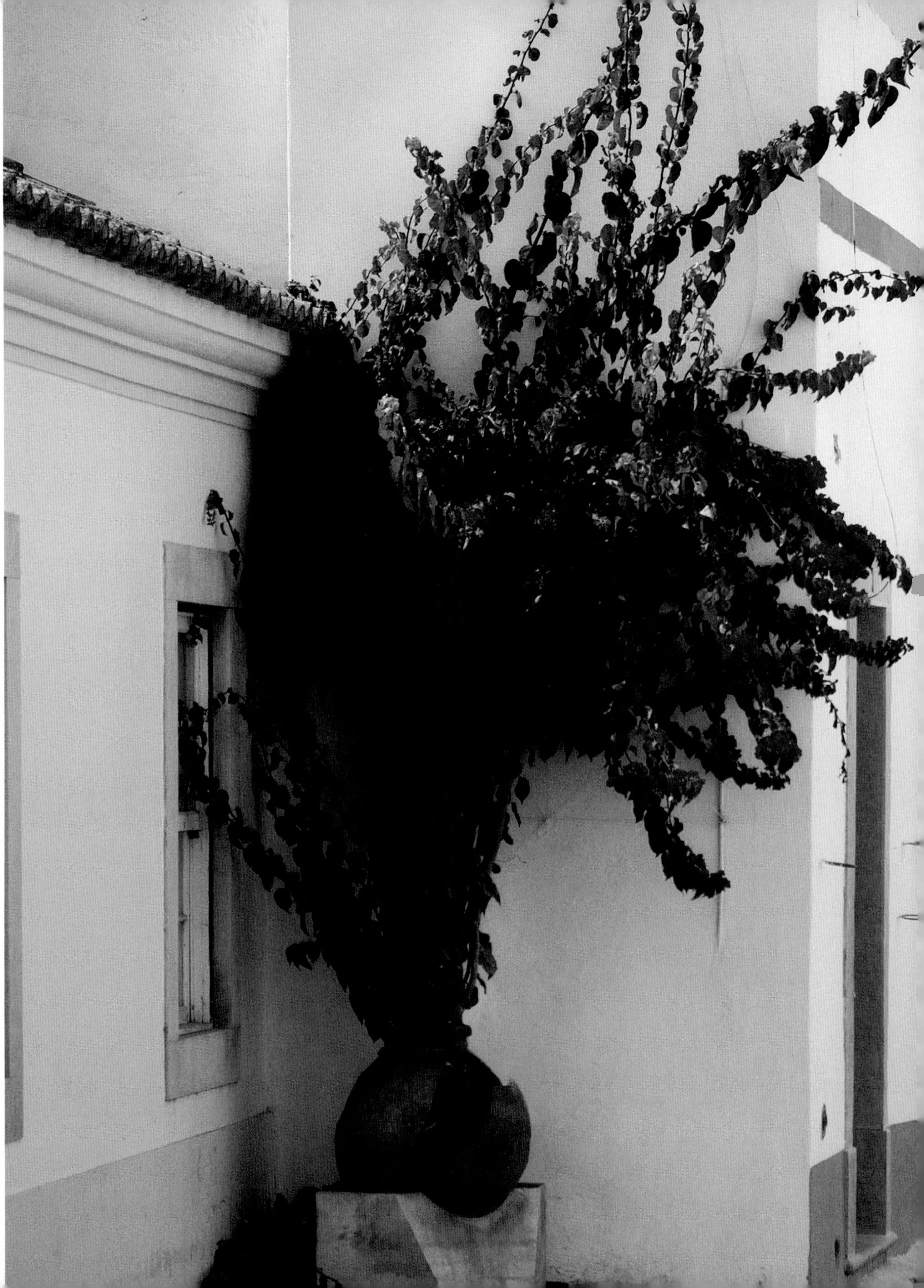

Opposite: Faro's narrow streets are picturesque and serene.

OPPOSITE: SILVES ENJOYS A LOVELY
NATURAL SETTING ON A HILLTOP IN
ALGARVE. A MOORISH CASTLE WITH
TWO TOWERS AND WALLS STANDS GUARD
OVER THE CITY, ONCE THE CAPITAL OF
THE ARAB RULERS OF THE REGION.
VISITORS ARE TREATED TO ASTONISHING
VIEWS OF THE SURROUNDING
COUNTRYSIDE.

OPPOSITE: A BRIDGE CROSSES THE
ARADE RIVER NEAR THE TOWN OF
SILVES IN THE FARO DISTRICT.
PP. 196-197: A PEDESTRIAN BRIDGE
CROSSES RIA FORMOSA NATURAL PARK
AND LEADS TO QUINTA DO LAGO BEACH.

OPPOSITE: A GUARDHOUSE IN RIA FORMOSA NATURAL PARK IN ALGARVE.
ABOVE: BOATS ON THE SHORES OF THE RIA FORMOSA IN ALGARVE.
PP. 200-201: THE ROMAN BRIDGE IN TAVIRA WAS ONCE PART OF A ROAD THAT RAN FROM CASTRO CARIM TO FARO.

OPPOSITE: ROCK FORMATIONS ON THE
ALGARVE COAST HAVE BEEN CARVED INTO
UNUSUAL SHAPES BY WATER AND WIND.

Islands

Madeira — The Azores

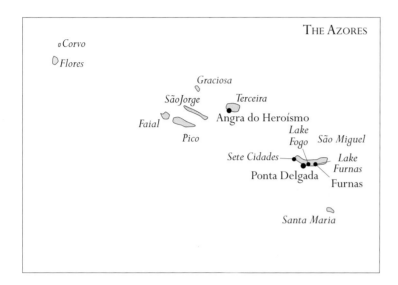

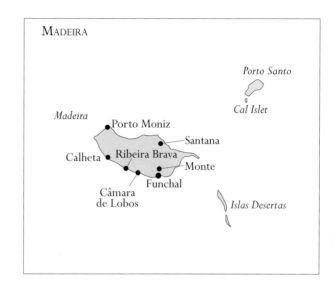

Madeira

Once an outpost of a long gone seafaring empire, Madeira and the Azores today are two of the jewels in Portugal's vast treasure of natural and cultural beauty. Madeira and Porto Santo, the two largest islands in an archipelago off the coast of Africa, boast soaring mountains and a mild climate. They are a lush paradise with subtropical vegetation. Species of plants were introduced here from all over the world, from Africa to the Americas, and they grow alongside native varieties in apparent harmony. Funchal, the capital of Madeira, dates back to the fifteenth century. Its harbor on the southern side of the island is simply stunning, and it is nestled in the embrace of a mountainous amphitheater. The buildings in the historic center are beautifully decorated; many have pleasant shady courtyards and architectural details in black (dark basalt) and white. Funchal has been nicknamed "little Lisbon" due to its resemblance to the larger national capital. The western coast of Madeira is untamed and spectacular. Small villages cling to the steep rock face, and terraced farmland dips precariously toward the ocean. Porto Moniz, though less than sixty-five miles (100 kilometers) from the capital city, feels completely isolated. Natural warm-water pools form in the rock along the water. To the south, nestled among vineyards and banana farms, Calheta gives off the sweet scent of the local rum, made from the syrup extracted from sugarcane that is grown here. Numerous fishing villages, botanical gardens, and charming rural landscapes dot the eastern side of the island. Just northeast of Madeira, the island of Porto Santo is flat and dry. This island was home to Christopher Columbus and his wife, Filipa Moniz. Local legend has it that Columbus dreamed up the idea of crossing the Atlantic in 1492 while staring out over the water here and observing the exotic and previously unseen vegetation that washed up on its shores.

205

P. 204: Rocky Cal Islet off the coast of Porto Santo in the Madeira islands.
Pp. 206-207: Câmara de Lobos, a fishing village on Madeira.
Opposite: In Porto Moniz on Madeira, natural pools have formed where the water carved away volcanic rock.

OPPOSITE: THE NATURAL WARM-WATER
POOLS IN PORTO MONIZ, MADEIRA.
PP. 212-213: THE COASTLINE NEAR
THE VILLAGE OF RIBEIRA BRAVA, ON THE
SOUTHERN COAST OF MADEIRA.

THE AZORES

The Azores are an archipelago of volcanic islands located far from the coast of Portugal in the North Atlantic. They are the result of millions of years of volcanic activity, and they are still shifting to this day. This exceptional geological formation has made the islands both strikingly beautiful and rich in natural resources. Hot springs, fertile soil, volcanic lakes, and lush vegetation all lend them a dreamlike quality. The largest and most heavily populated island is São Miguel, which has a green volcanic landscape. Its capital is Ponta Delgada. Numerous impressive churches, whitewashed houses, and convents for religious communities recall a glorious past, when the island was a stopping point for ships sailing from Europe to the New World.

The gigantic Caldeira das Sete Cidades crater lake is located on the northwest of the island. Seven and a half miles (twelve kilometers) in

circumference, it is surrounded by dense vegetation and two other smaller lakes. Lake Fogo and Lake Furnas on the eastern part of the island are also volcanic lakes. The latter is particularly active, and its warm waters remind visitors that geothermal activity is still very much alive on the Azores. In the nearby city of Furnas, thermal baths have been built to take advantage of the many naturally occurring jets of steam and spurts of warm water. In the fifteenth century, conquistadors occupied these islands; later military bases and weather stations were constructed on them. Today they are an autonomous region of Portugal, and their fast-changing and not overly sunny climate has protected them from mass tourism and kept them well-preserved. They are the westernmost stop in Europe on the way to more exotic lands. These far-off islands have remained secluded enough to preserve a daily lifestyle that moves to a quiet, gentle rhythm all their own.

P. 214, P. 215: MONTE PALACE ON MADEIRA AND ITS TROPICAL GARDENS.
PP. 216-217: FUNCHAL'S TOWN SQUARE IS KNOWN FOR ITS STARK
COLOR PALETTE.
OPPOSITE: THE TRIANGULAR HOUSES OF SANTANA ARE ONE OF MADEIRA'S
SINGULAR SIGHTS. THE WOODEN HOUSES WITH THATCHED ROOFS ARE
HUMBLE, BUT THEIR WINDOWS AND DOORS ARE PAINTED IN BRIGHT SHADES
OF RED, YELLOW, AND BLUE.

OPPOSITE: TYPICAL HOMES ON SANTANA, MADEIRA.
PP. 222-223: THE ISLAND OF PORTO SANTO, TWENTY-THREE MILES (THIRTY-SEVEN KILOMETERS) NORTHEAST OF MADEIRA DRAWS TOURISTS WITH ITS BEAUTIFUL SANDY BEACH.

OPPOSITE: THE CATHEDRAL IN ANGRA DO HEROÍSMO, A CAPITAL CITY ON TERCEIRA, AZORES.
PP. 226-227: THE WATER IN GIGANTIC CALDEIRA DAS SETE CIDADES CRATER LAKE IN NORTHEAST SÃO MIGUEL IS DARK GREEN.

OPPOSITE: THE LOVELY PROMENADE IN
PONTA DELGADA, SÃO MIGUEL.
PP. 230-231: THE AZORES ARE LUSH,
WILD, AND REMOTE.
PP. 232-233: THE WATER IN LAKE FOGO
IN THE CENTER OF SÃO MIGUEL IS A
BRILLIANT BLUE.
PP. 234-235: MUD AND MINERAL WATER
FROM THE HOT SPRINGS NEAR FURNAS ARE
USED AT THE MANY SPAS IN THE AREA.

OPPOSITE: GREEN HILLSIDES AROUND
FURNAS IN THE AZORES.
PP. 238-239: THE GREEN SHORES OF
LAKE FURNAS AND THE SURROUNDING
AREA ARE SIMPLY STUNNING.

Photo Credits

Printed February 2018 in China.